Nikki Gemmell is the author of nine novels and four works of non-fiction. Her books have been translated into 22 languages. She is a columnist for *The Australian*.

T0363396

On Quiet

Writers in the *On Series*

Nikki Gemmell

On Quiet

hachette
AUSTRALIA

Every attempt has been made to locate the copyright holders for material quoted in this book. Any person or organisation that may have been overlooked or misattributed may contact the publisher.

Published in Australia and New Zealand in 2020
by Hachette Australia
(an imprint of Hachette Australia Pty Limited)
Level 17, 207 Kent Street, Sydney NSW 2000
www.hachette.com.au

First published in 2018 by Melbourne University Publishing

10 9 8 7 6 5 4 3 2 1

A catalogue record for this book is available from the National Library of Australia

ISBN: 978 0 7336 4410 8 (paperback)

Original cover concept by Nada Backovic Design
Text design by Alice Graphics
Author photograph by Kathy Luu
Typeset by Typeskill
Printed and bound in Australia by McPherson's Printing Group

The paper this book is printed on is certified against the Forest Stewardship Council® Standards. McPherson's Printing Group holds FSC® chain of custody certification SA-COC-005379. FSC® promotes environmentally responsible, socially beneficial

All men's miseries derive from not being able to sit in a quiet room alone.

Blaise Pascal

I

I turn towards quiet like a plant towards the light. Yet stillness and silence—a recalibrating stopping—seem antithetical to how we live our lives now. We exist in abundance. We are drowning in a cram of rich living. Our cities are an agitation of the soul. And the simplicity of Blaise Pascal's longed-for room, with its rigorous demands, is beyond many of us.

Noise means a loud, unwanted, unpleasant sound. It is derived from the Latin word *nausea*, meaning seasickness. And so I drown. Needing the antidote of intentional quietude.

Quiet does not seek attention. It is an absence of bustle. It is a fervent wish for simplicity.

One of my favourite memories of living in London was when an ash cloud in Iceland stopped all the planes flying overhead for several discombobulating days. We didn't realise we lived under a flight path until there were no planes, suddenly, above us. There was noise, of course— all the regular noises of a city—but suddenly, crisply, the faraway noise that had accompanied us all our London days, for years, without us even realising, had gone. The world above us had, miraculously, fallen silent.

Quietude is the first leakings of dawn into the night sky. The golden hour at sunset when the world is exhaling and the light is honeyed up. It is flicking an off switch on the great noise of life. It is minimal, humble, spare. Quietude is the hand held to yours unasked. An eyelid tenderly kissed. A spiritual surrender. It is a release from worry and envy, from sourness and strop. Quietude is the sleeping infant in your arms. The house that awaits the return of the children, its breath held. The roar of the seashell to an ear. The hum of silence in the desert. The arresting communal stopping of a minute's silence at a football match. The pause; the necessary, listening pause. Quietude speaks to some yearning deep within us; a yearning for a replenishing peace. Quiet is strong. It is the observer and the listener, the distiller and the thinker. It is still. It is a gift.

The absence of planes in that London sky was odd and unnerving—there was just a clear, deathly quiet blue that everyone looked up to and marvelled at. Then gradually, into that silence, that vast sky-silence, emanated something akin to God. In our frenetic and faithless world it was arresting to experience; stilling and releasing. It quietened us Londoners. We no longer had to compete. We recognised the beauty in something else. And this new quiet forced us all to look around and observe our surroundings in ways we never had before.

The new urban quiet seemed eternally fresh. It constantly replenished itself and energised us all in days and days of exhilarating newness. And our ears felt like they repaired themselves, within the vast quiet, as did our grubbied souls.

Then real life returned. And we slipped back.

Quietude is not living in frustration, knowing you've never risked; but risking and failing, knowing you've at least tried.

Noel Coward, in his play *Design for Living*, declared that the human race is a letdown to him. That it thinks it's progressed yet it hasn't. That it thinks it's risen above what he calls the prime-val slime yet it hasn't. He said that we've invented a few things that make noises, but not one big thing that creates quiet. Endless and peaceful quiet—something that we can pull over us like a gigantic eiderdown, to deaden the sound of our emotional yellings and screechings.

How to find that eiderdown, how to rescue ourselves? It feels like a time for risky living; to glean tranquillity.

The quiet places are disappearing. Churches are being abandoned, rooms are cluttered and crowded, the bush is being logged; the contemplative places are vanishing from our worlds. What is this doing to our psyche? How is this agitating us in ways we barely know?

We need to experience quiet's bombastic opposite to truly appreciate it. Most of us exist amid cram; women especially. A crush of work in the home and the wider world, of family and of a myriad social snares, of life.

In *To the Lighthouse*, Virginia Woolf wrote about a state of longed-for quietude; a particular woman's state of grace where she did not need to think about anybody so that she could just be herself, by herself. Quietude was what this woman often felt the need of—to be silent, and to be alone. And in that moment, all the being and the doing, so expansive and glittering and vocal, evaporated. One shrunk, with a sense of solemnity, to just being oneself; something invisible to others, and free for the strangest adventures. It was a time when life sank down for a moment and the woman's range of experience seemed limitless ... her horizon seemed limitless.

A goal, that limitless horizon. A quietude that involves a surfacing into light, and lightness, which leads to an expansive unfurling of the mind. Allowing us to become unfettered, and from that we create. But how to revel in that limitless horizon?

Quietism is a word gaining currency. An old word, a new word, a possible movement for these troubled times. It means 'devotional contemplation and abandonment of the will ... a calm acceptance of things as they are.' It is softly doing the rounds in this fractious, bewildered, belligerent age.

Favete Linguis! Horace declared. With silence favour me.

The search for quiet was ever thus.

In quietude we become someone else. An earlier, simpler self. Absorbed, focused, lit; the childhood self. Happy in solitude, comfortable with it.

It's hard in this world to cleave quietude from our busy lives. Yet it is a compass into balm. For a lot of us it exists only on the edges and we have to journey to those edges to find it. But how?

The physicist J Robert Oppenheimer said that scientists 'live always at the "edge of mystery"—the boundary of the unknown.' And so can we all, on the cusp of quietude; for dwelling within it we are on the edge of mystery and release. We can feel the loosening in our shoulders and our neck and the softening of the clench in our face as we surrender to it.

The Guinness World Records has decreed a room in the US to be the world's quietest. It is an audio research laboratory at Microsoft's headquarters in Redmond, Washington, known as Building 87. It is a space where sound dies. The unnervingly silent room is known as an anechoic chamber—it's insulated from exterior noise but also absorbs all reflections of sound and electromagnetic waves. It is entirely echo-free. Microsoft explains that the room has the lowest sound ever recorded, and is the optimal environment for audio tests.

Can you imagine being placed in that room? With the lights off, all by yourself. Imagine the quietude.

Solace, or threat?

The hearing technology company Mimi has developed the Worldwide Hearing Index, an app that ranks cities according to noise pollution and hearing loss. It found that the average city dweller has an auditory loss equivalent to ten to twenty years older than their actual age. It's hard to find the silent sanctuary in our urban environment, but if you want a quiet city, the Index recommends Switzerland's Zurich. The Index identified Zurich as the least noise-polluted city in the world, based on the hearing ability of its inhabitants. No Australian city makes the top ten. The quietest cities were all located in Europe, except for Portland, in the US.

The cities with the most noise pollution are Guangzhou, then Delhi, Cairo, Mumbai and Istanbul.

An anechoic chamber at the Orfield Laboratories in Minneapolis held the Guinness World Record for the world's quietest room before Building 87 was constructed. You can book a tour of the complex, but visitors can't be left alone in the chamber for any large amount of time without supervision.

Journalists have visited this room. In the dark. Alone. Most lasted less than twenty minutes. They were tortured by the triumphant absence of sound apart from the noise their own bodies made. Owner Steven J Orfield says only two sounds are heard: your beating heart, which generates the gurgling sound of your blood moving, and spontaneous firings on your auditory nerve. Your brain is trying to seek out sound by turning up the volume of your auditory nerve, which results in high-pitched noises being heard. You hear the sound of your nerve working, valiantly, but you don't catch anything in the way of outside noise.

The quiet brewed by an Icelandic ash cloud made us yearn for it again. It unlocked something primal within many of us: a great stilling. That arresting time with our faces turned heavenward in wonder was talked about for days, months, even years afterwards.

Quietude is a haze of calming white. A kitchen anointed by sunlight. A candle's honeyed glow. The *Sanctus* in Fauré's *Requiem in D minor*. Emily Kngwarreye's desert washed by rain as well as Rothko's humming entrapment. The person clean of agitation and envy, anger and stress and strop. Quiet is the holy places. A fern-crammed glade, an abandoned church emptied of people, a desert's vivid silence. It is the intimate and the still, the mysterious and the contemplative. It is solitude, and a radiant contentment with that. It is the clean, shining hours and a tonic.

I need the medicine of quiet because noise is making me sick. The noise of the city; of motherhood; of work-stress. Of school runs and commutes and people endlessly asking things from me, depleting me, because I am not very good at saying no. It is the noise of bills that need paying and deadlines that must be met. The city where I live is never quiet enough to think in. The jackhammer yabber of the world is constantly in my head and at my fingertips.

And so I drown.

II

I have long held the opinion that the amount of noise that anyone can bear undisturbed stands in inverse proportion to his mental capacity and therefore be regarded as a pretty fair measure of it.

Arthur Schopenhauer

There is no firm anchor in a political sense, no balm of protection. Solid and stable governments seem a long time ago. Will those we entrust to protect us actually do so? We are not sure. Political disquiet is vining its way through our worlds. We worry that the hot-headed will rush us into wars we do not want, recklessly endangering us all; we crave peace and the hush of quiet and ego-less leadership.

'For though many instincts are held more or less in common by both sexes, to fight has always been the man's habit, not the woman's,' Virginia Woolf wrote. 'Law and practice have developed that difference, whether innate or accidental. Scarcely a human being in the course of history has fallen to a woman's rifle; the vast majority of birds and beasts have been killed by you, not by us; and it is difficult to judge what we do not share. How then are we to understand your problem, and if we cannot, how can we answer your question, how to prevent war? The answer based upon our experience and our psychology—why fight?—is not an answer of any value. Obviously there is for you some glory, some necessity, some satisfaction in fighting which we have never felt or enjoyed. Complete understanding could only be achieved by blood transfusion and memory transfusion—a miracle still beyond the reach of science.'

Is the female impulse an instinct towards quiet? Peace and serenity. A nesting. And is the male impulse an instinct towards conflict, belligerence, domination? Noise. War is noise. We live in an unquiet world and it will always be thus, with the testosterone-fuelled boy-men constantly tipping us into it. What is left? The quietness of mothers grieving their sons and unable to speak out loudly enough. The women drowned out by the noise of men.

Can quietude also be about women's rage? Women are not meant to be quiet. Our true natures are loud and sparky and stroppy, outspoken and stubborn and strong. But women are told from a young age to be quiet, obedient, neat. To reduce that roaring spark within us to something contained, controllable and blessedly tame.

Edith Wharton spoke of 'the curtain of niceness' that befalls young woman. Quiet is a tool of the patriarchy to silence, to render the female invisible, especially as they age. Women are consigned and bound to it from youth; when we are told repeatedly to still ourselves down into goodness. Politeness. Obedience. Perfection.

Forgetfulness is the new niggle of disquiet. Battle plans need to be drawn up to combat it because more and more often now there's the exhausting panic of *Where are my keys? Glasses? Phone?* I come into the kitchen—*Why am I here?* I find myself outside—*What am I doing here? It must be for a reason, but what?* This trouncing of order and calm is happening too often.

Is it age, the mothering of four children from kindergarten to the final year of high school, the stresses of full-time work, the constant harangue of disquieting news, of doing a million things at once—or is it something more sinister?

Religion scholar Sarah Sentilles wrote of plants, dubbed *escapes*, which spread beyond the area in which they have been cultivated, into an area where they've not been planted and do not occur naturally.

We all have a little something of escapes in us; the yearning for an escape into quiet.

Breaking news is now breaking my equilibrium. I wish I saw less of the fret-fest that is Donald Trump but I can't tear myself away from the compelling train wreck in my hand, on my phone. Research shows many of us are now spending almost nine hours a day logged onto a screen, more than most of us sleep.

The whoosh of news, too fast. Oh men, men, men. They shift allegiances in the playground, knife, name-call, spat. 'You're the king of the bedwetters!' 'You're too posh to push!' 'He has an emotional need to gossip, particularly when drink is taken.' 'There's a very deep pit reserved in Hell for such as he.' '*Et tu, Brute?*'

Meanwhile, no anchorage is firm, the iron is dragged on the seabed, lifting the people and casting them adrift. Screams and chaos, cries of doom.

No one is listening to us! No one is helping us! They're all out for themselves!

The sly intrusion of the internet is constantly at our fingertips. Are our smart phones eating our brains? Veering our sex lives into something different or non-existent? Changing how we work, socialise, sleep, stand and walk. Smartphones are our quietness-eaters.

Billions of dollars are being lost in productivity in US work places because of increasing addictions to phones. The staffing firm OfficeTeam found that US workers are spending an inordinate amount of time on their mobiles, gazing at screen morsels that have nothing to do with their jobs—so much rolling news to be checked, personal emails to be read and games to be played.

We are witnessing the digital drowning of an entire generation right under our noses. God help the children who've grown up with this, who have no memory of the spareness of the non-phone existence. No memory of the expansiveness of boredom. Of quiet. And what it brews.

The hot-headed are the old men who've waited too long, the prize in their sight but no grace in the seizing of it. Winning is all, but what about serving? What of the rest of us? We who are made to feel that we serve them, yet have not done it well enough. And so on they go and on; our leaders with their dirty work, their ambition polluting us all. It is vaulting cravenness laid bare. But fate is wily. Nothing goes according to plan. The wheel of fortune turns and turns again. And all the people crave is a haven to rest from the toss of the political world, yet no one is giving them one. Worry is not quiet.

The time of the women is coming. A cultural shift, a correcting, the want for the quietness of honesty and a steady hand. Yet how long will it take for these women, who feel like the future, to make change? They are islanded in their power and at a remove from the boys' club; the jostling, jockeying male spectacle paraded before us all; that peacock, belligerent, domineering strut when dignity flees, and grace.

It is possible to be a quiet leader, despite what the example of the world is telling our children now. There will be correction. We wait.

As women, let us not be quiet with our voices. Because by being quiet we are rendered invisible. Which is exactly what the men who are afraid of us want.

'Absent-mindedness is searching for the horse you are riding,' declares an old Russian proverb. Or, possibly, the glasses on the top of your head. Oh, the torment of this new brain fragility.

Defences have to be built to combat the forgetfulness; little scaffoldings of certainty to get you through the day. You enter the front door and your keys now have a regular home. If they go elsewhere, that elsewhere has to be paused over, noted, clocked. Because too often now a neighbour is ringing my doorbell to say I've left the car doors wide open, or my favourite shoes have been irretrievably lost because they must have been kicked off under a café table somewhere, and forgotten, and I walked home barefoot. The torment of disquiet.

Iceland's female prime minister, Jóhanna Sigurðardóttir, in response to Britain's Brexit referendum, quoted poet Ingibjörg Haraldsdóttir, who said that when all has been said, and when the problems of the world have been dissected, discussed and settled, a woman always arrives to then clear the table, sweep the floor and open the windows, to let out the cigar smoke. And that it never fails.

Mistakenly, I watch the film *Still Alice* starring Julianne Moore alongside two teenage boys. It is about a middle-aged linguistics professor with early onset Alzheimer's. 'That's you, Mum,' the boys josh at regular intervals. 'Alice! Alice!' is now their giggly taunt as my familiar refrain rings yet again through the house, 'Has anyone seen my purse, keys, shoes?' We jest, but this absent-mindedness feels like fallibility. The noise of the world is crowding in too much.

In the UK's Brexit referendum, the Leave movement won 'without a single bullet being fired'. So proclaimed its chief brewer of hatred, Nigel Farage, a far right leader who conveniently forgot Jo Cox. Cox was a Labour politician who was shot and stabbed by a man associated with the far right several days before the momentous vote—yet for the likes of Farage she had become a brief afterthought within the Brexit maelstrom. She shouldn't have been. She should not be vanished—relegated to obscurity—as history has shown us males are wont to do when it comes to women. We are banished into obscurity and silence; our quietness is insisted upon.

There are sneaky screen peeks in the dead of night, plops and pings of sleep-destruction and sudden flare-ups on our blue screens as they accept more fuel to torment our sleep even further or have us pounce, first thing, upon waking. Our poor brains; those saturated, fragile, exhausted, weakened vessels. Not only do smartphones addle sleep and work but also our self-esteem, reminding us of unquiet worlds we don't live in and relationships we don't have.

Bits and pieces of me are scattered everywhere, forgotten. Habits have to change, because too many details involving objects and names and places have sailed off to somewhere obscure. Milestone birthdays are attended alongside acquaintances from the distant past. *Who are you again? Cripes, did I sleep with you? Where do I know you from?* The disquiet in my head is too much.

Most distressing of all, in terms of the new forgetfulness, is the effect of the fracturing on my writing. And now I've forgotten the thought I had ten seconds ago as I veer off into the lure of the internet. The mind must become a steel trap to snare focus.

Writer Nicholas Carr, in his ominously titled book *The Shallows: What the Internet is Doing to Our Brains*, concludes that the grey matter in our brains is being rewired by the internet's saturation in our lives. Our brains change in response to our experiences. The printed book, according to Carr, focuses our attention and cultivates deep and contemplative thought. He argues that the internet, on the other hand, is remodelling our brains in its own image—promoting too much scanning and skimming and flitting.

The opposite of absent-mindedness requires quiet, calm, routine. Rush and panic crowd out sense, and that's when things get misplaced. I write in fragments for a reason now. Between them, I check the news on my unquiet phone, then drift off into something else. In panic I switch back and waste time trying to pick up where I left off; there's no longer the smoothness of unbroken focus; no longer a deep diving.

A fourteenth century Tibetan philosopher, Lama Je Tsongkhapa, said that emptiness is the track on which the centred person moves. As does the person who dwells within quietude.

A mate laments the rise of the smart phone because it's infiltrated all aspects of her life—including, most irritatingly, her boudoir. Not only does her beloved interrupt dinner parties with frequent, sparkling yet infuriating Twitter amuse-bouches, but he recently destroyed her intimate fortieth birthday dinner for two by concentrating more on his seductive new phone than on her. Then there's his biggest crime of the lot: the insistence on checking his screen during sex. His twitching at every seductive ping his electronic companion lures him away with. Which kills the moment entirely. Which makes her want to check her own phone. Which results in deeply unsatisfying sex for them both.

The female orgasm demands quiet. Quiet that allows concentration so a woman can slip off into another place; to catch it. For a woman to enjoy mind-blowing sexual pleasure she needs focus and commitment, to be utterly in the moment. The writer Simone de Beauvoir declared that 'sex pleasure in woman is a kind of magic spell; it demands complete abandon, and if words or movements oppose the magic of the caresses then the spell is broken.' And how ridiculously easy it is to dissolve that spell. The female path to orgasm is such a fragile, delicate one, and so easily lost. Our orgasms are shy to coax out, insisting on concentration and focus but also abandonment.

It takes time to surrender to quiet; to enter the sacred, exhilarating zone when we're jolted into life, combusted into light. The best sex involves a sense of connecting on the deepest level, with two people who are completely in the moment and focused.

I've learnt the danger zones that tip me into unquiet forgetfulness and have developed strategies to cope. I am mindful of moments when I'm easily distracted—when running late, when pressured, when not thinking straight—because that's when the mind-fragility crowds in.

I must find a way to live with more stillness now. Write down what used to be blithely remembered, clock changes in routine, take a deep breath and take note. Because I'm remembering the forgetfulness, and I am tormented by it.

A digital detox, out bush. The medicine of intentional quiet. A writing sojourn with no internet or mobile coverage. A necessary stilling and a reprieve from this saturated world. I was flooded by creativity and calm; I got my brain back when I thought it lost. I remembered the person I once was, pre-phone. More disciplined and focused, and more curious about my immediate surroundings. Screen removal gave me back control. Serenity and calm. The city world and all its distractions were washed off me and it felt like a huge and replenishing exhalation.

But how to retain that sense of exhaling? How to find a way of coexisting with it in the madness of everyday life? The impossible question.

III

Soon silence will have passed into legend. Man has turned his back on silence. Day after day he invents machines and devices that increase noise and distract humanity from the essence of life, contemplation, meditation … tooting, howling, screeching, booming, crashing, whistling, grinding, and trilling bolster his ego. His anxiety subsides. His inhuman void spreads monstrously like a gray vegetation.

Jean Arp

The writer Janet Frame wrote that 'people dread silence because it is transparent, like clear water, which reveals every obstacle—the used, the dead, the drowned, silence reveals the cast-off words and thoughts dropped in to obscure its clear stream. And when people stare too close to silence they sometimes face their own reflections, their magnified shadows in the depths, and that frightens them.'

The deadening hush of Building 87 reminds us that too much quiet can also be a threat. We are confronted with our own self and cannot cope with that.

There is a deeply humane beauty to communal quiet—a monk's dinner table, the Remembrance Day silence at 11 am on 11 November, that minute's silence at a footy match. Quiet is energised by its opposition to something else.

The dark is meant to be threatening. It's biological, something we've been conditioned against. Quietude is safe. The ultimate sanctuary. Yet I find quietude in darkness now; in a banishing of the incessant, busy, pushy artificial light that saturates our world.

'Stars only happen in videos,' declared my young son during our years of London living. He'd never seen stars from his home, nor the moon. London's night sky was bathed in a vast soupy orange and the familiar dark—that quiet, dense, rich, velvety inkiness of the countryside and deserts and remoteness and awe—never managed to find a foothold in his horn-blaring, brake-squealing, siren-filled urban world.

It was around then that my husband and I decided to come home, to Australia. To find quiet. A proper dark. To show our children that stars can exist in a city sky. And so we left that singular orange glow that obliterated all trace of an old fashioned night-time dark. We did it for ourselves, and for our kids. Yet we never quite found the proper dark in our urban life in Australia either.

When you immerse yourself in central Australia at night and gaze up at the star-scattered canopy above you it feels grounding, ancient, exhilarating; that the world is somehow righted. Whispering to some previous self, more attuned to nature and the oldest rhythms of the earth. True darkness feels like a balm now: precious, rare and silencing. Humans are evolving to not see darkness—proper, quiet darkness—as a threat.

'I see black light,' Victor Hugo declared on his deathbed. Would a black light be quiet? We all desire a death of quietude. My mother never got it.

The end of the world will not be marked by a bang but by silence. By a long exhalation. A slide into quiet. Akin to Building 87's quiet.

Night stokes our non-visual senses. A friend who's gradually going blind says that sex is getting better as her sight is diminishing. 'There's a great bonus in not seeing,' she laughs. 'You just relax. It's sex without ego.' And one of the most popular sex toys is the blindfold, of course. In darkness's quiet, the tenderness of touch can be electrifying.

Thomas Edison believed that the undeveloped being would improve under artificial light, and in the 1870s he developed the light bulb. But it cast a relatively gentle, benign glow compared to the forensic, intrusive light of the chilliest blue we're increasingly exposed to today. Inside our homes are cold light bulbs and blue screens that are far removed from the honeyed warmth of intimate candlelight. Outside, for city dwellers, are street lights and office lights and spooked lights flicking on at the slightest movement, condemning us to a permanent, unquiet state of non-darkness. Light pollution triumphs, colonising the far corners of our cities' nights.

I sleep with an eye mask because there's too much of light's insistence into the velvety dark and it doesn't feel healthy; it feels like an ancient, long lost body within us yearns for something more earthed and silent. An enveloping black now seems like a precious commodity. We're too awake in our screen and light-saturated world, our senses too alert when they shouldn't be.

Our innate fear of the dark has meant that light has bullied its way into wherever it can. Man has a noisy impulse to control whatever he can, which extends to the domain of darkness. We want to obliterate the dark just as we want to harness so much else in the natural world, whatever threatens or annoys or inconveniences us; whatever is in the way.

Our sleep is increasingly harangued by electronica's sly, demanding presence, the blue screens and blips; their noisome light. We've ceased to honour the quietness of darkness, its magic and mystery.

A car is a woman's shed. Quietude can be found in it, alone. Gunning down country roads with the windows down and the music up, with an elbow resting on the door, sun- and wind-whipped. A hand steals up, butting the breeze; the wind snatches an apple core. The road trip can brew such an uncomplicated, strong, pure happiness. The writer in me uncurls; there's no distraction, no demands, no rubbing out. It is dangerous, this. Too seductive and too removed from the unquiet world.

In the desert, quietude seems like an impenetrable mystery where God has uncurled upon this earth. In the luminously remote places, the silent and sanctified places, if you quieten and hold out your palms, perhaps the tears come,

perhaps. You may feel the hum of a wait-
ing presence—if you are quiet enough.

The dense quiet of a planted pine forest is
not quietude. It is threatening because our
hackles are raised, our wariness pricked;
the space feels too layered by loss. Ditto the
quiet in a nursing home's high-depend-
ency ward—it is the quiet of what could
be ahead of us. Then there's the concen-
trated hush of Building 87, reminding us
of a world without sound and of the terri-
fying aloneness, where all that is left is just
our heartbeat and our churning, unquiet
mind. And no one else.

Antarctica is one of the quietest places
on our planet and in summer one of the

brightest. Our largest frozen continent has never been permanently colonised. The emptiness is battering. Humbling. Diminishing. On a still day there's no sound of the wind, or restless water, or trees threshing in the breeze because there are no trees. The silence hums, the emptiness is penetrating. Closer to home, the salt pans of central Australia have a similar silence. And presence.

The scene: the local pool with a bunch of school mums, and my four-year-old is gently strumming her fingers through my hair. I'm yakking on about how I sometimes get so tired after school runs that I sit in the car outside the house afterwards, immobile, for five or ten minutes; in the lovely silence that doesn't talk back at me, in one huge and restorative moment of stillness.

These car moments are intensely therapeutic, and the women around me all agree we need them in our lives. We sink into companionable silence contemplating that little pocket of peace in the great rush of our days; mine made lovely by the fingers sifting through my hair like a tiny, tender rake. As if on cue, the fingers' owner pipes up: 'I think you've got nits, Mummy.'

Oh, for the soothing balm of a private car moment that instant. Everyone is laughing, and looking slightly aghast, and inching away as once again it's confirmed that I'm the woman who makes other mothers feel good about themselves. And the woman who craves the privacy and peace, the restoration and escape of her shed on wheels, too much.

Wild animals bring us into the shock of quietude. Coming across them unexpectedly, in the dark or the bush or even on a suburban street, you instinctively still. Contain yourself, quieten. You crave being in their presence, you want them close. Kangaroos on a suburban nature strip in Canberra. A flash of a fox on a moonlit round-about. Penguins stopped with curiosity near Antarctica's Davis Station. We have to still ourselves into quietude to connect, and to stir that ancient, long lost body that yearns, instinctively, for something else.

The feeling: *we're all in this together.*

Hic sunt dracones, or 'Here be dragons,' was the warning for seafarers on an old copper globe known as the Hunt-Lenox Globe, dated to 1510. The words are inscribed across the south-east coast of Asia.

Quietude is the opposite of that sentiment. It is the deep familiarity and certainty of home. It is the extravagant surrender into who you really want to be. And women—working women, mothers—so rarely get to be that.

Lieutenant William Dawes was quiet. A listener. He was the timekeeper in the early colony of Sydney—a quiet profession in itself. And in a series of tiny, fragile notebooks he recorded the *Grammatical forms of the language of N.S. Wales, in the neighbourhood of Sydney*. He did this by befriending a young Eora woman named Patyegarang. Dawes's notebooks are a meticulous chronicle of three months of contact between two very different people from two very different worlds. Dawes was able to establish a connection because he was quiet. He didn't coerce or impose. He listened.

I love going somewhere I've never been and a car allows me that luxury. It makes me think I can drink the world and it feels like my soul is unfurling in it. It reminds me of the woman I once was. Open, free, curious and earthed; quiet and receptive within exhilarating strangeness.

French sociologist and philosopher Jean Baudrillard said that 'driving is a spectacular form of amnesia ... everything is to be discovered, everything is to be obliterated.' As a woman, it's an empowering space where you're in control. Motherhood is about the loss of control; a loosening, a letting go.

There's little that is quiet about a loss of control. Being free affords you a quietness of the soul. Being in a car, alone, removed form the hubbub of regular life, affords a mother a quietness of the soul.

Sydney's founding Governor, Arthur Phillip, wanted to learn the language of the Aboriginal people to foster communication. He had several men captured, but most Aboriginal people were afraid to go into the colony's main encampment. Timekeeper Dawes lived in a small and isolated hut removed from everyone else. It was a safe place, a welcoming place, a place of quietness.

Patyegarang visited many times. She may have been Dawes's lover. Their relationship was characterised by quietness. She taught the Englishman the beautifully tender word *Putuwá*, which means 'to warm one's hand by the fire and then gently squeeze the fingers of another person.'

That is a connecting quietude, and so I try it, and yes, oh yes.

From Notebook B, page 34, Patyegarang: '*Nyímun candle Mr. D.*' *Meaning* 'Put out the candle Mr. D.'

From Notebook B, page 36, Dawes: '*Mínyin bial nanadyími?*' *Meaning*, '*Why don't you sleep?*'

Patyegarang: '*Kandúlin.*' Meaning, 'Because of the candle.'

The word *kandúlin is itself* quiet.

Occasionally I find myself in a church; Evensong in particular draws me in. There's something … all calming … about these deeply quiet, illicit experiences. A crack through the veneer of indifference; a gentle drip, drip, through the noise of busy life, the restlessness and the anxiousness. I feel 'righted' by these assignations, balmed.

As a nation, we need to listen more to Aboriginal people. William Dawes had the courage to be quiet. We all need to heed that lesson and be better listeners. Our national anthem encourages Australians, all, to rejoice. But we don't, do we, on 26 January? Not all of us. And as a nation that prides itself on a laconic sense of tolerance and inclusivity—a fair go for all—that's a problem. Because most of the people resolutely not joining in the rejoicing are the ones who were here first. Who are not listened to enough. Disquiet over the date is a murmur deep in our nation's psyche.

In the churches, these coracles of solace, I am brought down into stillness by a spiritual enveloping from a mostly sung service. I feel lit. As I do in the wild places, where the silence hums—Antarctica's ice desert, central Australia's sand desert, under a full butter moon. Sometimes I feel so silted up by the great rambunctiousness of city living. I am grubbied and depleted, and I need the cleanness of something hymnal. A tuning fork back into quietude.

Places of potent spirituality do not belong entirely to this earth. They are the sites that concentrate your being in some way, that soften your presence into something ceremonial and inclusive, with some echo of an ancient ritual embracing you.

Like the Aboriginal people who get sick if removed from their land, I crave the wild places of home, for they are my medicine for replenishing quietude.

IV

I sadly want a reform in the construction of children. Nature's only idea seems to be to make them machines for the production of incessant noise.

Wilkie Collins

Instinctively children are the *escapes*—plants that colonise places where they are not meant to. They surrender more readily to nature, and to the nurture of quiet.

For years I didn't have a mobile phone. I wanted to cave myself in quiet for as long as I could and I was fearful of how it would affect my writing. It was difficult to explain. 'How am I meant to communicate with you?' one friend barked. 'But your kids will never get playdates,' fumed another, 'we ALL text.' By this point this friend was shouting without realising.

The power of quiet is compelling in a child. Those that have mastered a withholding, a watching silence, are intriguing. Their stillness draws others to them; they're noticed. They're often popular in the playground, alluring, cool; others crave the gift of their attention. Quietness should not be perceived as weird or wrong;

it can be strong and self-contained, centred and courageous. The quiet children
feel like they absorb the most. They can
present themselves as the intriguing eye of
the storm, and I envy the poise of it.

It is possible to be a quiet leader. A quiet
doer. A quiet achiever. Despite what the
world tells us now.

One terrible morning a decade or so ago
I realised my world was too crowded. I
received three phone calls on the landline
just before bundling the kids into the car
for the run to two schools. The calls held
me up; I hadn't managed my breakfast let
alone the galvanising lipstick. My head
was swamped with impending playdates

and deadlines and I'd had too much wine at a dinner party the night before followed by a fractious sleep.

I bustled squabbling kids in the car and folded the stroller, smartly scrunched it down with a Blundstone-booted foot and hauled it into the boot. I heard a faint squeak. The stroller was responding. *Oh my God, my God.* I rushed it open to find a baby inside. Doubled over, stunned, her dear little back possibly cracked.

I've never held a child so fiercely. Trembling, I ran my hands over her body and skull. She was fine. The love, the horror, the guilt. Quietly I took a very deep breath, and strapped my precious baby into her car seat. Again and again, before my eyes, was that vision of a shoe curtly ramming the stroller shut; the sickening heft of it. And I realised that my life was too noisy, in too many ways, and this was endangering all of us.

I've been trying to clear the decks ever since. Learning the power of no: the release in the polite refusal. To reap the rescuing quiet.

In the cram of motherhood you lose who you are because you've given yourself over so completely to someone else. It's hard to find a quietude in that.

'Life should be touched, not strangled,' professed writer Ray Bradbury. It's particularly apt in this age of micro-managed parenting. Why is it so hard for our noisy modern generation to relinquish control of its offspring? To trust?

The NSW Teachers Federation has pleaded with parents to back off. They say a minority of outraged parents, with their sense of indignant righteousness, are creating chaos. Turning up uninvited during school hours; doorstopping teachers in class; yelling, bullying, even physically assaulting them. Where is the parents' sense of quiet containment?

I've heard a familiar refrain from various mums recently: 'I went mad.' With it comes a chill of recognition, for I have too, once or twice. I'm not proud of those moments, tangled up in the minutiae of my child's world. I am less that way now, mercifully, and I just don't enjoy the stew of the mummy madness anymore, where you're held hostage over some perceived unfairness, real or imagined. It's never been my better self; that person who's removed, sleepless and anxious, an outlier in their own lonely orbit and ridiculously unquiet.

Parenting experts blame the obsessive, noisy and hovering way of mothering on smaller families, which leads to increased expectations on their children, heightened anxiety about results and older, vocal mothers who are used to getting their way in the workplace and translating that to the classroom.

The quietness that comes with letting go what you cannot change.

Both a child psychologist and a psychiatrist I know mentioned, in passing, 'No one goes to church anymore.' Meaning, there's no communal guidance now for ways of behaving in a quieter way; no teaching a sense of how to be, which in the past led to an acceptance of authority and restraint. With our kids, we've never had so much freedom in terms of parental ways of behaving and thinking, and we've never clung on so noisily and so tight.

The child's will is like an eel, constantly slipping from our grasp. And letting go of them—to fail, to work it out for themselves—isn't always a sign of weakness but of its opposite, strength. You're releasing the other person but more importantly, you're releasing yourself. Into quiet.

Is it the loss of control that makes parents do it? Stress, or exhaustion or a feeling of sheer helplessness? Perhaps it's a combination of all three? Physically lashing out at our children, smacking them. Australia stands alongside the US in not banning smacking in order to send a clear message to an unruly child. But what kind of message is it?

It's about noisome stress. The sense of erasure the parent feels, immersed in a world that's constantly challenging, exhausting and blindsiding them—things not going their way, people not obeying their authority. When we can't control what we think is our right to, we get stressed—and colliding, sometimes catastrophically with that, is the loss of control that is parenthood.

It's a state of siege. I know that now. Mainly chosen, welcomed, revelled in, of course; but a siege nonetheless. Oh, for quietude's replenishing bliss.

It is a spare desk. A tidy house; everything neat and straight and in its place. I need order and calm to think. And every Monday morning there's a vast reordering of the house, into calm, after the whirlwind of the weekend's chaos. Only then can I sit at my desk and recalibrate with work. That makes me strong, spines me up.

Singer Adele, after having her baby, said that eventually she decided she was going to give herself one afternoon each week just to do whatever the fuck she wanted— without her baby. And that a friend of hers said, 'Really? Don't you feel bad?'

She replied that she did—but not as bad as she'd feel if she didn't do it. Adele explained that four of her friends felt the same way but they were too embarrassed to talk about it; they thought everyone would think they were a bad mum.

But that just isn't the case. Adele said it makes you a better mum if you give yourself a better time.

I feel like I'm living spiritually when I'm working; absorbed, focused, lit. When I can't glean the space to sit at my laptop, I feel fretful and angry, lost. The writer Gail Collins said that, for women, the 'centre of our story is the tension between the yearning to create a home, and the urge to get out of it.' It's her story, my story, the female story. The complex annihilation of motherhood.

The shiver of a thrill is as great as the arrival of the purple Malvern Star dragster I received, aged eight. Another such arrival enters my world, years later. In the Cabinet of Extraordinary Purchases that make up a life, this new acquisition is not glamorous, nor tender, nor beautiful. It is black and ugly and it squats in smug collusion under my desk, like an evil Death Star sucking all energy into its depths. It is a safe.

It transforms my life. Because it creates quietude in this house.

Long ago, my eldest, then a toddler, began a whiny tantrum. He wouldn't stop. I smacked him, which I'd never done before. He looked at me, bewildered, then burst into great howls of outrage. I rushed him into my arms and held him and held him, and wept, too: for what I'd done, and for the woman I'd become. I didn't recognise her. Stress had driven me to a place I'd never been. It was a like a rampant weed affecting every facet of my life, even the most cherished.

I'd never felt so depleted. As a freshly married wife with two small children I'd suddenly lost control of my world, the migraine-free existence of a single career girl who'd always called all the shots: what she ate, how much sleep she got, how much time she had to herself.

I'd been disappearing into the strange new land of the homemaker where I often forgot to eat because I was so busy tending to the needs of everyone else, where I'd sometimes end up crying over the dishes in the sink for no other reason than I was exhausted. I was dealing with a new diminishing; a feeling that all the promise and vividness of my youth, all its loudness and spontaneity and joy, was being rubbed out.

My safe is purely for one thing only. The objects that blight my existence. As a mother, I have turned into a woman I do not recognise, with a voice I do not like. The safe exists purely for screens.

This mysterious steel box is my children's distraction stealer. The jabbery-noise enveloper. My colluder in calm and quiet. The multiple screens have the ability to change the entire dynamic of our house and I cannot bear them, for what they do to my children and many kids around us. So now, for a large chunk of the weekends and nights, each child's screen is locked away. A quiet invades our world, and it is as wondrous as a house under a flight path where all the planes have disappeared.

The safe is my saviour because my four children were transported to Australia from England to be basted by fresh air and light, and that doesn't mean the electronic kind. Plus, I've lost more than a few devices over the years as ever more ingenious hiding places have been devised then promptly forgotten—and oh, the disquiet of that. (*Alice! Alice!*) Plus, long ago various children overcame the abject terror of the scariest place in the house—Mum's Underwear Drawer—to hold breaths and plunge and retrieve screens secreted away in it. Plus, I became sick of returning home from nights out to find a sloppy house; chairs nudging shelves and high cupboards ransacked; sick of hour-long battles over the blasted objects—because it felt too much like addiction. And I don't want teenage bedrooms violated by that rectangular glow late into the night. Their brains and bodies are growing; they need to be enveloped by a thick, womb-like, nurturing dark.

Kith is an old, quiet word, obsolete now. Yet it's often used in that expression of solace and return, 'kith and kin'. The word's original meaning: your land and your people; that which is deeply known and familiar. Jay Griffiths in her book *Kith* has looked at the way our western world is estranging its children from nature, and from quiet. From the earthy world of their early years, from the kith that sings so naturally in their blood and bones. We're evolving away from the natural world and Griffiths despairs of it.

The house's mood has been transformed by our safe. Its purchase was inspired by family holidays when a hotel room strong-box allowed us to quarantine screens from breakfast until evening. And we came together as a family, loosened, played and rediscovered each other. Bowed backs straightened, little faces opened to the world, tables hosted talk. Our family quietened. Wondrously. It felt soldering and strong.

Four kids down the track I haven't smacked a child in years, and I rarely shout; I've relaxed, let go. I've learnt that the threat of screens being locked in a safe, or a cancellation of the Netflix subscription, is a much more effective disciplinary tool. Discipline issues arise when you're failing to connect. They often feel like a child's extreme call for attention; the gift of noticing. Of listening. Of pausing. As a parent you need to reflect, take in, consider and communicate, and it's taken me years to understand that.

'My oldest childhood memories have the flavour of the earth,' wrote Federico García Lorca, a Spanish poet and dramatist. Don't we all have recollections of childhoods marinated in nature? Mine: tadpoles in jam jars; red-bellied black snakes in gutters; my brothers' red-back spider farm in ice cream containers in the carport; peeling paperbarks off trees; the dry flick of grasshoppers through tall grass; the summer shrill of cicadas rising and falling and then dropping into a silence, as crisp as an orchestra. It was an expansive childhood of wonder and freedom, rambling and daydreaming.

One night recently various kids held an unprompted, competitive piano jam. Composing and riffing, laughing and daring each other on. I sat secretly on the top step, revelling in the spontaneous creativity, cackling away like the old witch I was—the witch who'd spirited away all devices and introduced thick, non-electronic sleep into blighted lives; who'd deliberately sowed an old-fashioned boredom throughout the house. The chuff over this transforming, rescuing object feels as delicious as the mauve Malvern Star bicycle with plastic daisies on its spokes.

Writer Barry Lopez explains that the enervating joy of the natural world, discovered at a young age, can be a lifelong solace—and a fierce peace can be derived from this knowledge. Meandering days quietly basking in nature teach us autonomy and courage, risk-taking and self-rule—and respect for the beauty of the world around us. We learn those lessons in childhood, and carry them through life.

A theme of Jay Griffiths' writing is enclosure, the horror of it. Our children's worlds—with all the stresses of study and exams and the crowding of extra-curricular activities—are becoming relentlessly interior. Time is fenced off, boxed in; heads are bowed to screens; everything is compartmentalised. There is little sprawl. Griffiths argues that the way we're raising the current generation is deeply unnatural and children are becoming more fearful, depressed and dependent because of it; that unrecog-nised damage is being caused. She says the human spirit needs to feel quietly rooted, somewhere on earth, within the vivid green of our world.

It was obscene. Ridiculous. Wrong, wrong, wrong on every level. But oh, so right. I can barely bring myself to type the bare bones of this. My husband banished me entirely from the family equation. Disappeared me. Insisted, for all their sake. Sent me far, far away, beginning from that day of near-universal female collapse—Boxing Day.

How on earth could they survive without me? I flatter myself. They had a ball. The husband had planned this most particular dad-bliss for the one time of the year when work quietened for him; and he knew that they all needed a break from scary Good Cop, the House Disciplinarian. And I needed a break from myself. To be purged of the snapping and shouting; to become less cruel; and to sleep. In quietness.

We're fortunate in Australia because we can baste our children in nature without much effort—if we choose to. Awaken them to the wonder of the world around them, instil in them a soldering sense of kith. My daughter's preschool teacher described her as 'a true child of nature,' brimming with joy when she's getting mucky in the bush, climbing trees, cupping insects.

As a parent I have to honour that. Remind myself not to shut off the wonder of a fat butter moon and the roar of a sunset before nightfall bleeds in; to point out the oddness of a banksia and the beauty of a cicada shell. To pause, with her. Absorb quietly together the natural beauty we all take for granted. Because in adulthood she may well spiral back to it, and find a great solace in it.

The bliss of a temporary bed to myself. Mornings not rudely crashed into by a 5-year-old addicted to dawn. Going to the toilet without an audience—even the dog, most disconcertingly, has got in on that act. Bedtimes by 9 pm. A nit-free exist-ence. Cereal and or chocolate for lunch and dinner, too, if I want. Entire days without hearing 'Mum, Mum, Mum,' on wearying repeat.

It was one big Get Lost because the husband knew I'd come back stronger and calmer. It was creative oblivion and erasure and euphoria all in one and it felt urgent and necessary amid the drowning. And I highly recommend these restorative bouts, as essential therapy, for any mother screaming inside to find the woman she once was.

V

I hate the very noise of troublous man
Who did and does me all the harm he can.

John Clare

Shyness is the enemy and the bully. It ambushes me, the blush vining through my face; hot and impossible to halt. The reddened flush is a window to a mortified soul. It's the raw me, exposed; awkwardness laid bare. Hello to the frenemy that's been with me my entire life, that pulls me away from parties early; has me shrinking into silence at dinner tables where only the preoccupied host is known; has me mortified at the length of a charity debate I've foolishly agreed to do; has me dreading the school function where I have to walk in, alone. Shyness is the quietness that the wider world doesn't accept.

The power of the pause. That thinking silence between the slap in the face and the reaction. That moment between listening and talking. That rescuing stopping before countering, in heat.

Social and cultural historian Joe Moran says he's well qualified to write a book on the topic—called *Shrinking Violets*, no less—because he's felt shy for as long as he can remember. He worries that some countries are beginning to medically treat this deeply human vulnerability. Shyness, in some places, is now being diagnosed as a psychiatric disorder. Yet psychologists are pushing back, believing it's a move to 'correct' anything that falls outside the norm.

Do the socially awkward, who crave quiet, really need to be 'treated' by anti-anxiety drugs? Moran says he's torn. There are certainly extreme examples of shyness where people can't live their lives, but he thinks there's a trend to medically treat things that may well be within the range of human experience.

Socrates could enjoy a banquet now and again, and must have derived considerable satisfaction from his conversations while the hemlock was taking effect, but most of his life he lived quietly with Xanthippe (his wife), taking a constitutional in the afternoon, and perhaps meeting with a few friends by the way. Kant is said never to have been more than ten miles from Konigsberg in all his life. Darwin, after going round the world, spent the whole rest of his life in his own house. Marx, after stirring up a few revolutions, decided to spend the remainder of his days in the British Museum. Altogether it will be found that a quiet life is characteristic of great men, and that their pleasures have not been of the sort that would look exciting to the outward eye. No great achievement is possible without persistent work, so absorbing and so difficult that little energy is left over for the more strenuous kinds of amusement …

Bertrand Russell

Would you be aware of the shy people around you? Those of us so inclined often mask it well in the noisome world. I've not overcome my shyness yet have learnt to live with it. Hide it with social skills honed over the years, through sheer will; yet the blush still betrays me and sometimes with fellow blushers there's a veritable feast of reddened faces as we recognise in the other what we hate in ourselves, but cannot stop.

Shyness is about a loss of control—we like to feel comfortable, safe and quiet amid our surroundings. We can do close friends, one on one, small groups and prepared talks. We prefer listening to talking, asking questions to pontificating, writing to chatting, deep discussion to surface. That grand arena of small talk, the party, is often a shy person's hell, as are strangers thrust upon us and off-the-cuff talking in public. We need to prepare for the world. We don't like to be blindsided or exposed.

After extensive research, Moran found that shyness is far more common than he'd thought. Many people—often those he'd least expected—confessed to regular feelings of social awkwardness. Moran explained that one of the mistakes you can make when you're shy is to think that you're unusual in the way you're interacting—but that some of these problems are universal.

Devotion is a word to cultivate. Devotion to quiet. Creativity. Absorption. To the power of the pause. Quietude is grace; a hand hovering lightly at your back.

Driving into the city after sprawling days of writing solitude, I cannot bear to turn on the radio to hear the male sneerers that populate Australia's FM radio landscape.

The female simperers giggling and pro-
testing alongside them. Every new Donald
Trump affront. It's all so noisy and grace-
less and petulant. The barrage of the jab-
bery, newsy noise on the radio is draining
and cluttering and I slip back into a busy
life yearning again for those clean, simple
days out bush. When I felt washed of noise.

Virginia Woolf walking into a river in 1941,
with stones weighing down the pockets of
her overcoat, is the opposite of quietude.
It is soul agitation.

We have to stop worrying. It's white-
anting our serenity, crashing into our
lives. 'Today is the tomorrow you worried

about yesterday. Was it worth it?' Gandhi asked. Worry is the happiness eater. It is our taunter, exhausting and depleting us, crowding out far more productive thoughts.

A friend Helena embodied quietude. A doctor who'd worked for years in accident and emergency wards, she told me how colleagues of a certain age—middle-aged women, who've seen a lot of life and death—knew when the soul was leaving the body. They'd seen it often in the course of their work. Yet never talked about it with younger colleagues for fear of being ridiculed. But they discussed it among themselves, and recognised it.

Quietude is certainty. Living with uncertainty is the opposite of quiet. My mother lived with the extreme uncertainty of a chronic pain she could not control alongside an opioid addiction. Eventually, she committed suicide. It felt like a response to a consuming restlessness of the soul; a distressingly unquiet life.

Helena had mastered quietude. There was her stillness, as a gift, when she was with her patients in the last moments of their living; there was the quietness of her staying with them to give them company, and there was quiet, as their soul departed the corporeal body.

My mother's death was bleakly lonely and despairing. It was a distressingly unquiet death.

I saw Helena for the last time just before she boarded a plane to fly to Switzerland, to kill herself. She had booked herself into Dignitas, a clinic for assisted dying, after living for twenty-four years with chronic pain. The bullying pain was triggered by a chest virus in her late thirties and over decades the discomfort had spread throughout her body. Helena had tried everything to fell it; she was now heading towards life in a wheelchair. Repeated surgery hadn't helped and her careful administration of opioids only provided temporary relief. She had four children who had all reached adulthood when she made her decision. They had been with her every step of the way.

My mother wanted the peace of mind of some kind of euthanasia, some form of legally assisted dying. In the end, she couldn't wait for any laws to catch up with her. No one, friends or family, knew she was going to kill herself. She died with the noise of uncertainty, and pain, and helplessness, and despair. The noise of being ignored by the world as an elderly woman.

My last coffee with Helena was determinedly celebratory; suffused with a quiet knowing. It was time, she was ready, and in a week she would be dead. She wanted to celebrate. The last time I saw her she had a face of radiant certainty. A radiant, peaceful, ready certainty; beautiful in its quietness. It was a death not of despair, but release.

The act of euthanasia gives a person who wants some form of assisted dying agency. A sense of control. Peace. A quietude to live a life of sprawling delight in the final months, and to die a good death.

You are at once both the quiet and the confusion of my heart; imagine my heartbeat when you are in this state.

Franz Kafka, in a letter to his fiancée, Felice

Sprawl is such a beautifully relaxed, jovial word—but how to cultivate it? Because from the looseness that is sprawl comes a quietness of the soul. Les Murray's deeply Australian poem 'The Quality of Sprawl' makes me realise how far, as a nation, we've drifted from it.

'Sprawl is doing your farming by aeroplane, roughly, or driving a hitchhiker that extra hundred miles home.' Murray writes that it's also the bloke who cuts down his Rolls Royce and turns it into a farm ute, but then again sprawl is most definitely not the company that 'made repeated efforts to buy the vehicle back and repair its image.' There's a laconic cheekiness to sprawl, an endearing larrikin energy that's selfless and smart.

In a near-Orwellian world, manufactured fear is the way to control. And it feels as if we're in the midst of a worry epidemic right now, thanks to the chest puffery of the bullyboy shirt-fronters. Will they be the death of us all? Our nation's millennials are succumbing to the worry bug most of all—they've been crowned the world's most miserable. Or, perhaps, the most unquiet in terms of their interior life.

A Deloitte Millennial Survey looked at data of young people across thirty countries and found Australians aged between 18 and 35 are the most pessimistic of all about their future prospects. They're jittery about the way their country's being run and worried about job prospects as employers veer towards the cruelty of the casual and freelance position. They're fearful of an increasingly tense planet in these heckling dark times, as races and religions jostle for hegemony. And only 8 per cent believe they'll be better off financially than their parents. They believe they'll never own their dream home.

Sprawl was Bob Hawke declaring a national holiday after the country's America's Cup win and the dazzle of Paul Keating's invective. Sprawl is playful, which those who fear change never are. Sprawl is captivatingly individual, never the lemming-like leanings of the robotic and fearful herd. Sprawl is not the Australian customs officials who officiously destroyed 200-year-old plant samples from France before the email exchange was exhausted. It is flexible and easygoing, genial. As Murray explains, 'It is the rococo of being your own still centre.'

The fractiousness of the world is right at our fingertips now, tweet by instant tweet. Ever-present screens crowd danger into our thoughts 24/7 from all corners of the globe. 'How much pain they have cost us, the evils which have never happened,' Thomas Jefferson once said. I spent much of my teens niggled by the stress of potential nuclear annihilation, watching the nuclear clock inch ever closer to midnight. And did it happen?

Sprawl is most magnificently exemplified by the 12-year-old boy who drove 1200 kilometres from the NSW mid-north coast to Broken Hill, on his way to the relos in Perth, before he was pulled over by the cops. Sprawl is also the police who decided no conviction would be recorded and the matter would not be going to court. Sprawl is journalist Mark Colvin's final tweet declaring 'It's all been bloody marvellous' hours after his death. As Les Murray says, 'It is loose-limbed in its mind.'

Sprawl is not the haters knotted in their fury crowding the Twittersphere. Sprawl is not clenched. Not loud. And not Twitter. It's the dog curled like a comma on the pub verandah with 'No Food' spray painted across its back, not the sign 'No Public Toilets Here' on the servo after a wearying six-hour trip. Sprawl is never, ever banks. It's not being tutored from kindy so you can pass selective-school entrance exams seven years later—sprawl is not going to get too far in this hot-housed world. Or is it? There's something to be said for emotional intelligence in our young, and the quality of sprawl has that in spades.

Worry is joy-denying. Exhausting. Depleting. We can and should train ourselves out of worry. You can feel the souring drag that fret and stress have on you. The sky is not going to fall in. As Winston Churchill said, 'When I look back on all these worries, I remember the story of the old man who said on his deathbed that he had had a lot of trouble in his life, most of which had never happened.'

'[Sprawl] listens with a grin and one boot up on the rail of possibility,' Les Murray writes. Note, it listens.

We have lost the quality of sprawl. There's too much anger now, too many people who don't have time for it, and that's an Australian tragedy. People might argue that our nation can't afford the quality of sprawl in the world that we live in now, but I say this quiet and lovely quality will save us.

VI

I was quiet, but I was not blind.

Jane Austen, *Mansfield Park*

Why practice the lost art of recital? To cultivate a love of literature. To boost self-confidence. To improve the speaking voice. To exercise the brain. To glean quiet.

Novelist Will Self declared dinner parties should last only ninety minutes. Because he doesn't drink, he gets bored. He doesn't mind people drinking as long as they aren't falling over. A stance I whole-heartedly concur with because the wolf-ish hunger for solitude is lean and mean within me.

'I feel a real horror of people closing over me,' Katherine Mansfield declared. It's a horror that yowls inside whenever too many noisy demands nibble into your serenity. And the ability to cleave precious moments of quiet from within the great whoosh of family and professional life is becoming increasingly difficult. The ulti-mate social nightmare? A party far away, in a place devoid of taxis, fully reliant on someone else for a lift. Someone who lingers, agonisingly, over one more drink and anecdote, the bloated evening yawning on.

Solitude is never overcomplicated, stressful or loud—and it most certainly is never lonely. You can be much lonelier in the midst of a family Christmas, or within a marriage that's atrophied into indifference. Aloneness can have a vast restorative power; there's something spiritual and consoling to it. There's space for your mind to uncurl.

Trapped in holiday land. Which means four kids at home practically climbing the walls because of an endless dreariness of rainy days while one struggles to hold on to a career with the words of Katherine Mansfield, in the thick of trying to write, hovering in one's head: a mind full of the ghosts of saucepans.

That mind clanging with the guilt of unused cooking implements was what Mansfield believed working women were constantly living with. A sentiment relevant to the question of whether women can be artists and mothers at the same time; and, if they dare, whether they should limit their domestic ambitions to a single child. Because motherhood is just so darned noisy.

Artist Tracey Emin, childless, has no regrets. She said she could never be a mother and a good artist because the emotional pull would be too much. Author

Lauren Sandler declared women should restrict their families if they wanted to avoid limiting their careers. She highlighted a remark from Alice Walker about female artists having only one child. Walker had declared that with one you can move, but with more than one you're a sitting duck.

A sitting duck. Too close to the bone. But I'd be a far worse mother if I wasn't working. Cagey and restless, raging and roaring with unfulfilled ambitions—and taking it out on the kids. I write because it releases me. Into quiet. As a mother you're at the coalface of living, which is a great place to be as a writer, but work firms me—buoys me—amidst the great loss of control; the grand disruption to routine, equilibrium, energy, self.

I gravitate to a tiny sliver of space in my house to meander with thoughts and work, and to observe the lovely heft of the seasons. As soon as I saw the high verandah, *heard* its quietness, I knew I finally had a room of my own. The quiet place. But like everything else in this cacophonous, brimful life the rest of them had other ideas. The tin lids gravitated to my little sanctuary; taking turns to sleep on the old cane daybed every night for its canopy of stars in the city and its curtain of lovely sound. And for its witching hour, when the space is anointed by a tranquil, golden, deeply Australian light.

During my London years there was a corrosive yearning for the terrain in my blood and bones. And I realised it's not only Aboriginal people who hold a monopoly on a profound and spiritual connection to this land—the craving can addle any of us. Our landscape is a vast seduction. Within it I feel more like the person I once was; a freer, lighter, less agitated, quieter childhood self.

So I gravitate to this little verandah with its wondrous curtain of sound, and when I'm on it I'm like a lit candle. The journey to get to this verandah in front of a national park is the most beautiful and strange in my life, because it's about coming home. It's about paying attention to detail with an outsider's eye yet a heart born in this place. I've always been a neophiliac, hungrily seeking the new, yet now, bizarrely, it's all changed. And I'm content. With this, just this, the deep familiarity of home.

In the lovely, glittery alone a door opens to possibility. It's when novel ideas sneak in and titles roar with their rightness and surprising character arcs veer you back into excitement over a project that hasn't been singing. It's a brewing house for creativity; my Laboratorium of Wonder. Plotinus called it 'the flight of the alone to the alone,' yet as a mother it carries an enormous burden of guilt.

Mothers shouldn't feel guilty about working but we often do. What we mustn't be doing, as women, is conveying that sense of guilt to our children. They need to see pride and chuff about female employment; they need to experience the quietness in our souls that work affords us.

You can't do it all, be it all, within the rush of modern motherhood; something has to give within that great, exhausting triumvirate of family, work and social life. Yet the clincher, as precious little jewels of alone are gleaned, is knowing that the more solitude you can filch from your days, the less you will shout later on. At everyone else. Within the thick of motherhood the restorative power of aloneness feels like a private miracle. It's when things get done.

Is it just me or does the social world now feel a little more shouty, in your face, per-formative? Everyone's so eager to talk at you—but to actually, quietly, enquire of you? To listen to you? Is the art of con-versation morphing into something else? Demonstration. Display. Rant.

We're not listening. Deeply connecting. We're skimming and flitting too much. Aristotle said wise men speak when they have something to say, but fools speak because they have to say something.

Novelist Marilynne Robinson describes herself as 'a solitary,' yet tempers it. She says her solitary life is not exclusively that; she likes to come out and look at the world and talk with people, but it's a matter of balance. I, too, scuttle out into the world for the odd party or dinner where my car's close, for escape; but I've become more courageous with slipping off, unobtrusively. It's my strategy for survival. The aim, to exist in quietness. So I can be better with everyone else.

The film director Mike Nichols, renowned US broadcaster Diane Sawyer's husband, said that one of the things that fascinated him about his about wife's work, as she travels all over the world, is that no one ever asked her about what she saw. Nichols knew that people, by and large, would rather be talking, than listening. Even to someone like her.

Learning by heart is a form of mental exercise. It demands quietude. Leave the skill untended and the ability rusts away. And like handwriting and shoelace tying and listening, its significance is fading. Memorising anything at length now is an agility, a marvel, that's being lost amid everything instantly on tap; screens are constantly at the ready for whatever we want, slicing into our focus and thoughts.

American *Vogue* editor Anna Wintour is legendary for lasting twenty minutes or so at a party and then vanishing, a technique I've perfected with hosts none the wiser. The child wails loudly 'Are we there yet?' at the promise of the new destination, the adult wails inwardly 'Are we there yet?' at the promise of home.

The golden hour. An Aussie beach. An evening of clearness, a gift to us all. Several families around a fire. The glow sticks are losing their potency and the sparklers have all burnt down—whirly gigs and words in the sky, too brief. The world is settling, exhaling at last. Suddenly, a voice. 'There was movement at the station ...'

Arrestingly, within the softening light. The entire *Man From Snowy River*, all 104 lines by heart. One by one we listeners are reeled in, caught; especially the children who've never heard of the colt that got away, never sat before the galloping rhythms of Australian recital. There's a shine in the speaker as he sits there quietly and stuns us all.

A TEDx talk. They're meant to be memorised; it's a feature of the tightly controlled rules of presentation. But the words in my noisy, scattered head feel like they're hanging on by their fingernails. Mortified, I surrender to palm cards. Memorising is a lost skill of quietness. My mind refuses to relax and absorb. I will my brain to astound me and resolutely, disappointingly, it does not.

Patricia Highsmith said her imagination functioned much better when she didn't have to speak to people.

Poets are big on recital. Joseph Brodsky demanded his students memorise a thousand lines per semester. To prepare them for later life, he reasoned, for whatever might be flung at them. And to provide solace. During his own forced exile by the Soviets in the Arctic he was grateful for every piece of poetry he had in his head. Politician and writer Aung San Suu Kyi exercised her memory during her own long imprisonment by learning a new poem every day. In the end she'd memorised Tennyson's and Yeats's complete works. The moving quietude, in all of that.

The words of Banjo Paterson wash over each intently listening adult with a great calm of reverie and wonder. 'Mum taught me as a kid,' the reciter shrugs quietly afterwards, sifting his fingers through the beach's sand. 'I've never forgotten.'

VII

The house was very quiet, and the fog ... pressed against the windows like an excluded ghost.

E M Forster, *Howards End*

I've never been fond of architect Le Corbusier's maxim, 'A house is a machine for living in'. I prefer 'a house is a mooring for living in.' A place that gladdens your heart as you step across the threshold; that releases you into a space where you can be your true self. A sanctuary of stillness amid the great gallop of life. Simplicity is key.

In winter's clench the less reluctant I am to venture forth. Pour me into the flannelette sheets, tunnel me into the warmth. Oh, the horror of the event-packed week. The bliss of the dinner with friends cancelled at the last minute and it's not you who's done the cancelling. And I get twitchy if a night out is more than once a week.

This is how I was as a child. Hated being forced into the noisy glare of Going Out, being told to act jolly and put on the mask. Do we become more like our younger selves in middle age? Perhaps, for some, yes. This is disconcerting yet deeply familiar. Not so much that I've found myself, finally, but that I recognise myself; a long lost person who's now crawled out from under the rubble of who I was trying to be, for so exhaustingly long. Well hello, you find yourself saying to a 10-year-old self, I remember you. And just as you've let go, as your life's loosening and light- ening and quieting with age, and you couldn't give a damn about being anything but yourself.

Just as you can glean an insight into a person's psyche—in all its ugliness or beauty—in an unguarded moment with a dog, a person's attitude to a garden is like a door flying open into who they really are.

Virginia Woolf's last diary entry before committing suicide: 'L. is doing the rhododendrons.' There's something so moving about that, a woman looking out for her husband, knowing that life goes on, *will* go on, in all its order and quietness; and that solace and connection will be drawn from that. The couple had a steady rhythm of work, garden, work; both needing that regular circuit breaker of earth and air after a desk's intensity. What did Leonard do after Virginia's body was discovered, three weeks later, in the River Ouse? Garden. The next day, for the entire day. No doubt drawing a quiet solace from it.

This feels like a returning. I taught myself in adulthood how to be in the world, but perhaps through decades it was a weight somehow burdensome and now I'm slipping back into the ease of who I really am. I feel found. It's a huge relief. That I don't have to be who everyone else wants me to be; that I can be who I want to be. Quietly. In middle age I can shake the world off.

Peace is drawn from my tiny patch of earth. When we first moved into this house the soil released its secrets over the coming year and I learnt. Noting exuberant little cackles of colour blooming in odd corners, unfolding freshly week after week, so thoughtfully planted by unknown hands. There was the thrilling pageantry of it all, and a gratitude for the person who once loved this garden so much.

My symphony of wonder. The shy white camellia bush tucked in a corner. Heady jasmine blaring the arrival of summer. The cascade of sudden bougainvillea. Blousy hibiscus. Bullying bamboo, overbearing and intent. The first, thrilling, gardenia. A puckish West Australian flowering gum. We'll quieten you yet, it all seems to be saying—astonish, delight you, smile you up.

I need the earth. I lived apartment-high in my twenties yet it felt tetchily too far from the soil and the trees, from the singing green; dizzily detached and unsettled. At one stage I lived in a tiny London mews house that once stored Portobello Road Market carts and I drew endless delight from two exuberant window boxes, our sole patch of green. I tended to them as lovingly as babies. In England I planted a slender gum, so pale and silvery and shy, amidst the robust British greens in every back garden that we had.

The joy, now, is to exist simply and quietly. To be with children veering too quickly into adulthood. Every day they seem a little more removed from our orbit, particularly the teenage boys. They're so beautiful, these child-adults before us; cusped so precariously and ever more unknowable. And I never see them raucous in the outside world now, loose and large with their mates; that goofy, risky, beautiful tribal world of intense loyalty and fat happiness.

As we age we experience an inexorable drawing towards nature. A desire to enfold ourselves quietly back into the sights and smells of our own childhoods, when we lived closer to the sky and the earth. The anaesthesia of the known: that's what the modern exile often flees from. We are all *escapes* to some extent.

Yet there comes a time for most of us when we want to reconcile with the known. Corrosively. And now I have returned to a cascade of Australian, childhood green. It's incalculably restorative.

A nun I know says that people bless houses, spaces and rooms that they abide in with their energy, their presence, and their soul. Anyone can be the sower of that blessing, religious or not. And it can be the opposite scenario, of course; a dwelling can be a place of sourness and disquiet that can mirror the inhabitant's soul.

The last words of George Orwell's domestic diary, as he lay in bed with lungs bleeding: 'Snowdrops all over the place. A few tulips showing. Some wallflowers still trying to flower.'

As we near death there can be a softening to quiet wonder as we note the beauty and resilience of the natural world around us. We are moved in a way we are not when younger. It's the great, endless turning of the plants—all the little miracles of creation, stoicism, obedience—that will still be there, presumably, long after we're gone.

A new bliss: sending my teenagers GIFs, animated videos of several seconds' duration. They turn into the infuriated disciplinarian trying to control the glee-brimmed child. It is Ultimate Embarrassing Mum, and endless joy. It is connection, and as a mother of teenagers I crave that in any way I can. I can't do GIFs on a night out so might as well stay in. Which I do, most often, drinking in the replenishing quiet like a draught. Watching the children grow, marvelling at their catapulting into being grown ups.

And happiness these days is not so much those big noisy waypoints in life—births, birthdays, weddings—but in the spaces in between. The small moments, like the arrowing of a GIF into a teenager's phone, and the watching, in quiet wonder, for a return. They'll never know how much joy that incoming missive gives me—a silent little implosion of bliss, tight in my heart.

Inventor and entrepreneur Steve Jobs knew simplicity's potency. 'Simple can be harder than complex: You have to work hard to get your thinking clean to make it simple. But it's worth it in the end because once you get there, you can move mountains.'

Planting trees has significant health benefits. Researchers in Toronto have found that having ten or more trees lining your street has cognitive and psychological benefits similar to being seven years younger.

The researchers compared satellite imagery of trees and health data. Team leader psychologist Marc Berman said that people who live on tree-lined blocks are less likely to report high blood pressure, obesity, heart disease and diabetes. But they can't pinpoint why. Berman wondered if it's the trees cleaning the air, or encouraging people to go outside and exercise more, or if it's merely, wondrously, their aesthetic beauty.

So to the wonder, for me, almost every morning. That sure path into quiet—a walk in the bush. Tree-brimmed, glad of heart, as I stride into the city of birds. An everyday exhilaration, but it has to be alone. I don't want anyone else's chitter chatter and mind swamp and twig snap. I need the free alone.

I can feel myself straightening within it. The posture correcting, the back uncurling, with a hand on a scribbly gum's cool trunk and the thick vellum folds of the paperbark and a face strong to the sky. This is what it is to be alive. Connected. Quiet.

Someone close to me has lived in a succession of council flats over the years, and with every visit the heart flinches at the noisy soullessness of these places; they're concrete boxes of the depleted human spirit. Why no rampant green? Why is the tonic of the tree not instinctively recognised here, that invigorating shot of nature? For these fragile people—of all people—it seems like a relatively cheap life-enhancer.

The poisoning of the mighty trees is not unknown in these parts, and every time a council sign draws attention to the fact I'm enraged at the sheer selfishness of the communal transgression. It's an almost spiritual rebuke, a soul retraction. What are we doing? The natural world too often bears the scars of our noisome short-sightedness. As Wordsworth lamented, 'I have learned to look on nature, not as in the hour of thoughtless youth; but hearing oftentimes the still, sad music of humanity.'

CSIRO researchers have coined a most beautifully quiet word for a familiar smell in our thirsty land. *Petrichor*. The distinct scent of rain in the air. Or more precisely, the name of an oil that's released from the earth into the air before rain begins to fall. It's derived from the Greek *petra*, meaning stone, and *ichor*, which is the blood of the Gods in Greek mythology. That intoxicating smell of the earth opening out to receive its benediction is the most intoxicating smell of all and never fails to give pause; to still one's soul into quiet.

Our great good place is often connected to childhood, if not physically then in memory; it is the stirring of some happiness from long ago like a Chinese whisper of solace. There's something spiritual in the urge to embrace a homecoming as we age; the way we're quietly drawn back to the places where we began. It is the great circularity of life, and it's often acutely connected to landscape.

'We wove a web in childhood, a web of sunny air,' Charlotte Brontë wrote and how beguiling that sounds, how understandable the want to recapture the sheer, unadulterated happiness of childhood, the very air of it. The shift of its seasons, insects, light. What quietness of the soul did these childhood immersions in nature give us?

The Libyan revolutionary Muammar Gaddafi was captured in his childhood town of Sirte. There's something intensely human and vulnerable about the idea of the besieged man, on the run, returning to where he began. Marilynne Robinson wrote in her novel *Gilead* about loving a town so much that you think of going into its ground as a last, wild gesture of love.

Great good places often involve that quiet, humble, undervalued quality: simplicity. They're almost ridiculously anti-material-ist. Shining hours in simple places, with not much in the way of furniture or pos-sessions; sometimes just a swag in a desert by a certain tree, in a cherished riverbed, a secret place where the silence hums. Life is a process of simplification. A stripping back to unearth the seam of quiet.

Writer John Bunyan said that if we have not quiet in our minds, outward comfort will do no more for us than a golden slipper on a gouty foot.

The word quiet derives from the fourteenth century French, meaning 'peaceable, at rest, restful, tranquil.' It is directly from the Latin, *quietus.*

At rest. A necessary luxury.

The only way to soothe an agitation of the soul is to acknowledge it, and to stop pretending that everything's alright. I've tried controlling it by simplifying my life— saying no, more often, and not feeling guilty about it. And by having a bath at night to ease me into sleep. And by filching some restorative pocket of 'me' time every day, somewhere in the day. And by never getting to that point again of wanting to smack my child. And by surrounding myself with positive people, which has meant distancing myself from some friends who've flattened me repeatedly over the years; I've found the courage to say no, enough, I want to be surrounded by heart lifters not heart sinkers; for the opposite gives me an agitation of the soul. My love for my family is weighty, voluptuous, all-consuming, and I have to glean some kind of quietness amid everything— for their sake, as much as mine.

For a quiet existence, turned like a plant towards the light, this I have learnt: That a life driven by love is preferable to a life driven by greed or ambition. That it's wise to distance yourself from people who want to flatten you. That forgiveness is releasing, for yourself most of all. That kindness is life-affirming. That the most intense happiness is to be found in the simplest of things—the sight of your father laughing uncontrollably during a film, a bedroom filled with the sleep of your children, requited love. That a turning to quiet feels like a turning towards authenticity. That a great solace, and stillness, can be found in faith; it helps you to let go. That at the end of our lives the question should not be what have we noisily done, but how well we have loved.

By writing this I have found a way into quiet. Because it is doing what I really want to do. By writing and thinking about quietude, I have slipped myself into it. And am released.

Quietude is about shedding. Simplifying. Listening. Saying no to the noise. Quietude is holy whether you believe in a God or not. You are paused. With a radiant certainty. The gigantic eiderdown is pulled over you, finally, and you rest. Do you aspire to become a reaper of the quiet?

It rescues.